"Never That!"

It's All In The Way You Play!

By
MARION P. MYERS

ILLUSTRATED BY PIERRE BREVARD

To order additional copies of this book, contact:
Xlibris
844-714-8691
www.Xlibris.com
Orders@Xlibris.com

Book Designer: Jerome Cuyos

ISBN: Softcover   978-1-4257-4108-2

Print information available on the last page

Rev. date: 10/28/2020

To The Parent/Teacher:

Welcome to the "Never That" series for children. This series specifically focuses on character/value education traits. When these traits are introduced and nurtured at a young age, a child can cultivate healthy critical thinking skills and social skills. Character/value education promotes an awareness of what is good, wanting good, and doing good. These traits are exemplified via experiences that children encounter in their everyday lives. It is an excellent source for spending quality family time together. This series can be used for guided reading, read alouds, or self-selected reading. There are activities in the back of each book to enhance reading and language skills. Remember: Words open new vision and horizons. A better world begins when our children can read with comprehension and enjoy reading.

The character/value education traits in this story are fair play, courage, responsibility and kindness. Mario did not show fair play during the spelling game when he wrote the words on paper because he did not follow the rules of the game. Alicia showed courage when she told Ms. Walston someone was cheating even when Marsha refused to tell the truth. Duane and Jonathan had to be responsible when monitoring the refreshment table. Mr. Keys demonstrated kindness when he gave the new students his other gifts.

Marion P. Myers

It was a windy day. Trees were blowing, leaves were flying and the sky was cloudy. It looked like rain. There was a heavy overcast in the city. It was the kind of day that made you feel gloomy. But for the students at Delan Middle School and Bell Elementary it wasn't gloomy at all. The schools were next to each other. It was the last day of school before the Christmas holidays. Nothing could bother the students in the least or so they thought. Teachers planned parties to celebrate the holiday. Cheer and gladness were in the atmosphere.

"I'm so glad it's our last day! I can't wait!" Duane exclaimed to Jonathan as they got off the school bus. Their hands were full with bags of chips, cookies and presents for their teachers and friends.

"Yeah, I'm glad too, now I can sleep late, play my games and just chill," Jonathan responded.

"Me too. Alicia will be trying to beat me at my new games my mom is getting me, I keep telling her that I am the video king, undefeated!" Duane bragged as they walked to their lockers.

Meanwhile, Alicia was having her own fun at school. She was helping her teacher set up for the party.

"Ms. Walston, we sure got plenty of food. I hope I fixed enough cupcakes," Alicia said.

"You did sweetheart and they look good too," Ms. Walston responded. Just then, Carl looked up and started to cough and grabbed his stomach.

"What's the matter with you?" Marsha asked.

"Uh, uh, I don't want to get sick off of Alicia's cupcakes!" Carl chuckled.

"Well, never that you don't have to even eat them," Alicia said indignantly.

"That's right, more for us," Marsha agreed as she gave Alicia a high five.

"Okay, okay, let's keep it nice, Carl, you will not participate if you keep making remarks like that," Ms. Walston replied.

"Yes mam, I was only joking."

"That's not a nice joke," Alicia retorted.

The bell rang and it was time for class. Everyone was bringing their contributions to the room. It was full of delicious aromas.

"Good morning. I know you are all excited about our party and this being the last day. After I check the roll, we will play a spelling game. There will be no cheating; if you are caught cheating you will not participate in the party. Is that understood?" Ms. Walston said sternly.

"Yes Ms. Walston," The class answered in unison.

"Also I have some great prizes for those students who get the most points."

"What kind of prizes, like what?" asked a student.

"You'll have to win to see. Let's get started," Ms. Walston answered.

You couldn't hear a pin drop. Everyone was ready to play. They had to clear their desks and divide up into two teams. The rules of the game were explained and questions were asked.

"All minds clear?" asked Ms. Walston.

"Bring it on!" screamed the class.

The game was going well. Team "A" was down by three points. This was the last chance for them to make it a tie.

Each word was worth three points. It was Mario's turn to spell the word 'captivity'. The class was extremely quiet.

"Come on Mario, make us winners!" his teammates yelled.

"Shut up and let me think," Mario responded.

"Watch your mouth, don't use that, say, be quiet instead," Ms. Walston answered.

"C-A-P-" as he was spelling the word, Marsha saw a piece of paper hanging out from one of team B's player's desk with all the words written on it. Someone had written them each time a word was called out so the next person to spell could look at it. She motioned to Alicia to look at the paper. Alicia gasped. They both knew that team B had cheated. Yes, they cheated all during the game. It was terrible because Alicia wanted her team to win. And she was on team B. As for Marsha, her team, team A was loosing but with the discovery of cheating going on, team A would automatically win. What would Alicia do? What should she do? It's almost certain that Marsha would tell Ms. Walston. Or would she? After all she wanted her team to win. Marsha and Alicia were best friends

and she knew if Alicia's team won, she'd share her prize with her anyway, right? So why tell? Alicia whispered to Marsha,

"Tell Ms. Walston."

"No, you tell her."

"No, you saw it first."

"But then I'll be picked on and called a snitch. Nobody will like me or want to play with me then," Marsha said sadly.

Alicia shook her head and said, "Never that, I'm your friend. I wonder was it Carl who did it because he's the best speller in our class, next to me."

Marsha looked puzzled. She knew the right thing to do but didn't want to do it. All of team B would hate her because they couldn't participate in the party.

"I can't do it Alicia and I won't do it," Marsha whispered emphatically.

"Well, I guess I will and I will tell Ms. Walston that you saw it and then told me."

"You're going to put me in it?"

"You *are* in it!" Alicia said abruptly.

"Then we'll both be picked on."

"Never that, I'd rather tell the truth," Alicia replied.

"But, you know how it goes, every time someone tries to do the right thing, they get bullied by the other students," Marsha said.

"That won't happen this time," Alicia responded.

The game was tied. Team B was next when all of a sudden the fire drill bell rang.

"Oh no, it's our turn!" yelled team B.

"Let's settle down. Line up and be quiet," Ms. Walston instructed. They walked to their designated place in the yard and stood in absolute silence for fifteen minutes. Later the school principal signaled for everyone to return to class.

"Now is the perfect time to tell Ms. Walston what happened," said Alicia.

"No, I just can't do it!" Marsha exclaimed.

Just then, Alicia started to tell Ms. Walston what happened. She became very angry but assured Alicia that she would not disclose who told her. Ms. Walston couldn't wait to get back to class. She was not just angry but very disappointed in her students. After everyone went to their seats, she walked over to the desk only to find not one but two cheat papers. The class was in shock. It was at Carl's desk. He was the captain of team B. Somebody tried to make it look like Carl had done it because the team captains were in the front of the class. Carl looked stunned. He was speechless.

"Carl I know you didn't do this, you were in front of the class during the game. You were team captain. The handwriting isn't even yours. Someone has set you up Carl," Ms. Walston announced looking at the class with disgust.

Everybody looked at each other. Who could it be? Ms. Walston looked at the words and randomly had various students to write some of the words on the board. She found out who did it. She knew who cheated.

Before she said another word, she looked at her class. She looked again and then asked,

"The person who did this can come forth now or I will call you out. What will it be?" Just then, in walks Mr. Walston with the pizza Ms. Walston had ordered.

"Hi boys and girls. I know you're ready for your party. This pizza is sizzling hot!" he said.

"Thank you for bringing it. But you know, we have a problem," Ms. Walston informed him.

"What?! A problem, what do you mean?" Mr. Walston asked.

"Someone cheated during the spelling game. Here's the proof." Mr. Walston looked at the paper with unbelief.

"No, not this class. They wouldn't do that," he responded.

"Well, they did," Ms. Walston answered sadly.

Ms. Walston's husband was as shocked as she was. He didn't think that anyone of them would do such a thing. The class was still quiet. You could even hear the next person breathe, it was so quiet. Then all of a sudden, Mario raises his hand.

"Ms. Walston, uh, urn, uh, I know, well, I know who, uh, I did it."

"Who, what you did it Mario?" some of the students yelled.

"But why would you help the other team to win and not your own?" asked Marsha.

"And why did you put it in my desk?" Carl asked.

"I wasn't trying to make team B win, I tried to make team A win and then I slipped the paper in somebody's desk who was on team B. That way, it would look like they cheated if it was found."

Mr. Walston walked over to Mario and put his hand on his shoulder, then sat down to talk.

"That was brave of you Mario to come forth and tell the truth and admit that you were the one."

"I'm sorry but nobody on my team even looked at that paper. No one did and that's the truth. I'm sorry Ms. Walston. I just wanted to win so bad that I did the wrong thing. I wrote the words out for myself and I know it's against the rules. I probably would have shown it to anyone who was having trouble," Mario pleaded.

"Yeah and I bet your team members would have jumped at the chance to use it too," Carl remarked.

"No, no, never that, none of us need to cheat, Carl," Alicia answered.

"Mario, I'm not going to call your mother because I know you feel really bad for what you did," Ms. Walston remarked.

"I'm sorry team," Mario said.

"But you will not participate in the party," Ms. Walston replied.

"I know, I know," Mario answered.

"Son, you learned your lesson. Maybe you can help me load up the car," Mr. Walston said.

"Okay, I will," Mario answered solemnly.

The party went on as planned. Everyone was having fun even Mario. He was helping Mr. Walston pack Ms. Walston's car. She was cleaning out her room.

Marsha was amazed at how it all turned out. She looked at Alicia and said,

"You were right, nobody will pick on us."

Alicia smiled, "Marsha, no, never that!"

Meanwhile, Duane was having some drama at his school. They were having a hall party. Each grade had their own music, food, and games. Certain students were asked to monitor the refreshment tables. Duane and Jonathan were two of those students. The halls were loud with laughter and cheer. Dance lines were formed. Teachers were patrolling the halls. Duane went to the room to get more sodas. When he returned, his table was cleaned. Some students had come by and grabbed all the food.

"What happened, where did all the food go?" Duane asked.

"What, where were you?" Jonathan asked.

"Remember I told you I was going to the room to get more sodas?"

"Yeah, but I had to go down the hall to get some more plates and cups. I only left for a few minutes," Jonathan answered.

"Just enough time for *anyone* to grab all the food that was on my table," Duane replied.

"But Duane, you were in charge of *your own* table."

"I know, but Mr. Keys is going to be so angry," Duane said.

"Look, here he comes now," Jonathan said.

"Hey, how's it going, looks like you had a hungry crowd Duane? Go get some more snacks for your table. We've got so much in there," Mr. Keys said.

"Okay," Duane answered.

"Jonathan, you go and get some more too. I'll watch the tables."

"Duane, see, you didn't have anything to worry about," Jonathan assured him.

"Maybe I should have waited until a teacher came before I left. It wasn't your job to watch my table," Duane responded.

"But you asked me and I did but when I went down the hall that's when somebody got real greedy and took the food."

"Yeah, well we know what to do now plus there's so much food to serve, there's enough for everybody."

The party ended and it was almost time to go home. Each class had to clean up. Paper and food were all over the hall. The floors were sticky from spilled sodas and candy. Some students tried to dodge from cleaning up but Mr. Keys made sure they did their share. After the clean up, gifts were exchanged. Everybody got something, well almost everybody. The new sister and brother who just transferred did not get gifts. Mr. Keys didn't want them to feel left out. They started school last week but were absent everyday except today. He wanted them to feel like part of the class. He was very relieved that his

wife packed some extra gifts. He called Duane and Jonathan to come and get a gift for each of them.

"Merry Christmas," Duane and Jonathan said.

"Merry Christmas to you. Thank you," the sister replied.

"Thanks," said her brother.

That night Duane and Alicia talked about what happened at their schools. They both talked so much that Ms. Corbett had to tell them to slow down and go one at a time. Each had a real story to tell. But they all missed Dad. He died three years ago of a heart attack. So the holidays had many special memories mixed with sadness and joy.

"And I thought you both wanted to stay home on the last day of school before the holidays," Ms. Corbett laughed.

Duane and Alicia looked at each other and grinned, as Alicia said, "Never That!"

Pre-Reading Activity

These questions can be asked before you begin the story. The child can relate his/her experiences to the story. They can make predictions and inferences as they read and discuss the story. The child can answer these questions verbally or write their answers.

1. What is your favorite holiday? Why?
2. Do you do special things during your favorite holiday?
3. How do you feel when someone cheats in a game?
4. Are you a responsible person? Can your parents, teachers, or friends depend on you?

Story Elements

What are story elements? Story elements are different parts of a story that make a story complete. They are the plot, setting, characters, theme, problem, solution, tone and mood.

The plot is the goal of the story, what does the character want to accomplish? Alicia wants to tell the truth about who really cheated during the game.

The setting is where the story takes place and the time. This story takes place at Alicia's and Duane's schools. It takes place just before the Christmas holidays.

The characters are the people in the story. The characters in this story include Alicia, Duane, Jonathan, Mario, Carl, Ms. Walston, Mr. Walston, Marsha, Ms. Corbett, and Mr. Keys.

The theme is the main concept the author is writing about. In this story, the author is conveying concepts that include fairness, courage, responsibility and kindness.

The problem is the trouble in a story. In this story, the problem is Mario's cheating and whether or not Alicia and Marsha will tell the truth and be confronted with ridicule by their fellow classmates.

The solution is the answer to the problem. Alicia solved the problem by telling Ms. Walston what happened during the spelling bee.

The <u>tone</u> is the way the author writes a book. What kind of words are used?, are they sad words, happy words? Does the author write a funny book, a mysterious book, a sad book?

The <u>mood</u> is the way you, the reader feels after reading a book. Do you feel happy, sad, confused?

<u>Open Discussion:</u> Allow your child to make comparisons from the story. For example, what makes Alicia and Marsha different when they were both aware of Mario's actions?, compare how they each respond. Draw conclusions and make predictions by addressing the events that occur in the story. What could have happened if Marsha did not tell Alicia about Mario's cheating? If Alicia had not come forth with the truth, would they all be guilty of cheating-Mario, Alicia, and Marsha? How would Duane have reacted if Mr. Keys found out he left the table unattended? What would Mr. Keys do or say if he did find out?

<u>Complete a Story Map:</u>

This can be done using different colors of construction paper for each element; have the child to write the name of each one and write a sentence about each one on the paper.

This can be used for other stories also.

<u>Post- Reading Activities:</u> Ask the child to write about the story. For younger children, have them retell the story and draw a picture from the story. Ask specific questions- What is the name of the story? Who is the author? Who are the characters? Where does the story take place? What is the story about? Did you like the story? What would you have done differently? Have you ever experienced anything like this in your own life?

STORY MAP

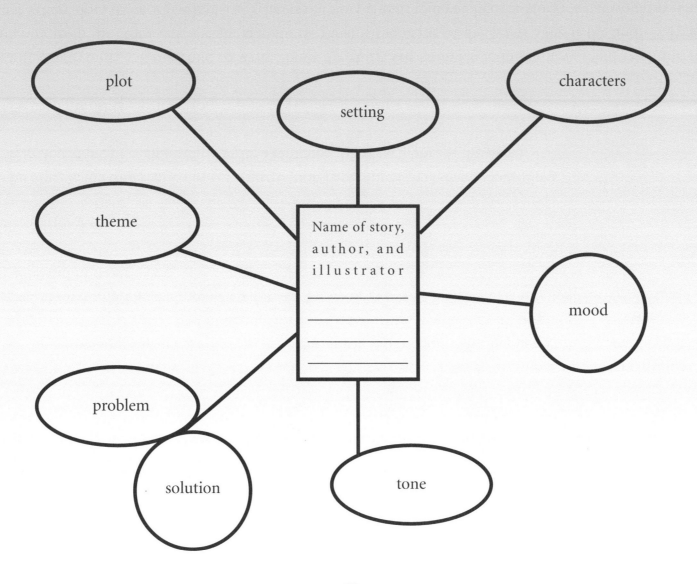

Printed in the United States
By Bookmasters